INDEX

The Islamic State's Model

The Islamic State announced several months ago that it was "annexing" territory in Algeria (*Wilayat al-Jazair*), Libya (*Wilayat al-Barqah, Wilayat al-Tarabulus and Wilayat al-Fizan*), Sinai (*Wilayat Sinai*), Saudi Arabia (*Wilayat al-Haramayn*) and Yemen (*Wilayat al-Yaman*).

It is likely that the Islamic State plans to pursue a similar approach in Afghanistan and Pakistan following its announcement of accepting pledges of allegiance from former members of the Afghan and Pakistan Taliban to also try and "annex" territory there under the framework of a new wilayah called "Wilayat Khorasan."

On its face, this bold declaration of an expanding number of wilayat (*provinces*) resembles the announcements by al-Qaeda of creating numerous franchises in the mid-2000s. The Islamic State's "wilayat" strategy differs in significant ways from al-Qaeda's "franchise" strategy, however.

The academic literature has shed great light on the al-Qaeda franchising strategy. Typically, affiliates joined up with al-Qaeda as a result of failure. Affiliation helped with financial support; offered a potential haven that could be exploited, along with access to new training, recruiting, publicity and military expertise; gave branding and publicity; and opened up personal networks from past foreign fighter mobilizations. It in turn helps al-Qaeda with mission fulfillment, remaining relevant, providing access to new logistics networks, and building a new group of hardened fighters.

But those franchises often became as much a burden as an asset as local interests and views diverged with those of the parent organization. Al-Qaeda increasingly came to view franchising "warily" in part due to its inability to always control its new partners such as Abu Musab al-Zarqawi and al-Qaeda in Iraq as well as because of backlash from unsuccessful cooptation of organizations such as the Libyan Islamic Fighting Group or Egyptian Islamic Jihad.

This is one of the reasons why, prior to Osama bin Laden's death, the Somali jihadi group Harakat al-Shabab al-Mujahideen was not given franchise status. Bin Laden had apprehensions about the group's utility due to past clan infighting and lack of unity. Following the death of bin Laden though, his replacement, Ayman al-Zawahiri, brought Shabab into the fold, but the results have been quite disastrous; Shabab has declined and also was in an internal feud between its foreign and local members.

There is one key difference between al-Qaeda's and the Islamic State's model for expansion. Al-Qaeda wanted to use its new franchises in service of its main priority: attacking Western countries to force them to stop supporting "apostate" Arab regimes, which without the support of Western countries would then be ripe for the taking. This has only truly worked out with its Yemeni branch, al-Qaeda in the Arabian Peninsula (AQAP). On the other hand, while the Islamic State does not have an issue with its supporters or grassroots activists attacking Western countries, its main priority is building out its caliphate, which is evident in its famous slogan *baqiya wa tatamaddad* (remaining and expanding).

As a result, it has had a relatively clear agenda and model: fighting locally, instituting limited governance and conducting outreach. This differs from al-Qaeda's more muddled approach – it hoped a local franchise would conduct external operations, but many times franchises would instead focus on local battles or attempts at governance without a clear plan, as bin Laden had warned.

Moreover, the Islamic State has had a simple media strategy for telegraphing what it is doing on the ground to show its supporters, potential recruits and enemies that it is in fact doing something. This accomplishes more, even if it appears that the Islamic State is doing more than it actually is, in comparison with al-Qaeda's practice of waiting for a successful external operation to succeed and then claiming responsibility after the fact.

So far, Libya and the Sinai appear to be the locations with the most promise, though the Islamic State's presence in these areas should not be overstated. It certainly does not command the amount of territorial control as its base in Mesopotamia. That said, the Islamic State's wilayat in Libya and the Sinai are following the same methodology on the ground and in the media as the Islamic State's wilayat have in Iraq and Syria.

By contrast, its wilayat in Algeria, Saudi Arabia and Yemen have yet to show any signs of activity. It is certainly possible that the Islamic State is playing a long game and preparing its soldiers and bureaucrats for future jihad, governance and dawa (*propagation of Islam*), but there are reasons to be skeptical as well. Following Islamic State leader Abu Bakr al-Baghdadi's announcement of the expansion of the Islamic State, its media apparatus took over the media departments of all the local wilayat outside of Mesopotamia. This highlights that, at least on the media level, the Islamic State is in full command and control.

In Algeria, there were some signs of action that have since petered off. The leader of Wilayat al-Jazair, Abd al-Malik Guri (*Khalid Abu Sulayman*) was killed by the Algerian military. Further, while northern Algerian-based jihadis have certainly conducted attacks over the years, they have had a difficult time operating or conducting sustainable campaigns that have resulted in gaining territory. Moreover, there have been no signs that Wilayat al-Jazair has conducted any military operations since it beheaded the French tourist Hervé Gourdel, which was prior to the Islamic State accepting the group into the fold. It has also not been involved in any type of governance or dawa activities.

There have also not been any formal military or governance activities carried out by the Islamic State's wilayat in Saudi Arabia or Yemen. The Saudi government claims the Islamic State was involved in an attack that killed several Shiites in al-Ahsa and Islamic State supporters claimed responsibility for an attempted assassination of a Danish businessman through a drive-by shooting on a highway in Riyadh. The Saudis have a history of dealing with insurgency against al-Qaeda on its territory from 2002-06 so are ready for any fight if the Islamic State attempts to start a campaign there.

As for Yemen, AQAP is the strongest jihadi presence and took major issue with Baghdadi's announcement of creating a wilayah in Yemen. AQAP's top sharia official, Harith al-Nazari, released a video rejecting the Islamic State's claims and calling for the dissolution of all groups so as to pledge baya (*religiously binding oath of allegiance*), stating: "*We reject the call to split the ranks of the mujahid groups*" and "*export[ing] the fighting and discord [in Syria] to other fronts.*"

As a result, although there are indeed some supporters of the Islamic State in Yemen, they have yet to show any sign of activity. It is possible that the jihadi dynamics in Yemen might change after the Houthi coup, but unless the Islamic State is able to take the reins of the AQAP apparatus from the inside, it has an uphill battle due to AQAP's roots going back a decade. Therefore, it is unclear how the Islamic State hopes and plans to operate in those environments.

This leaves the Sinai and Libya as the primary models for the Islamic State's expansion. In the first six weeks since Baghdadi's announcement, it appeared that the Islamic State in Sinai was continuing to operate in a similar manner to how its predecessor in name Jamaat Ansar Bayt al-Maqdis was acting by conducting attacks against the Egyptian military as well as gas pipelines. Since the beginning of 2015, there have been small signs of an expanded program including elements of Islamic State governance present elsewhere. For example, Wilayat Sinai burned marijuana after detaining drug traffickers and it distributed funds to residents of Rafah after the Egyptian military demolished their homes to create a buffer zone near the border with Gaza.

On top of these inchoate steps, similar to the promotion of Syria and Iraq as lands of opportunity for locals and locations for foreign fighters, the Islamic State has pushed similar narratives regarding the Sinai. When Baghdadi made his announcement he stated that *"we ask every individual amongst them to join the closest wilayah to him, and to hear and obey the wali [governor] appointed by us for it."* This further push illustrates the seriousness of this endeavor for the Islamic State.

First, its semi-official media agencies al-Battar and al-Jabhah al-Ialamiyyah released the pamphlet *"Come to the Sinai to Elevate the Foundations of Your State,"* by Abu Musab al-Gharib, which echoes Baghdadi's call. Further, the Islamic State's official anashid (*religiously-sanctioned a capella music*) and Quranic recitation outlet Ajnad released a nashid titled *"The Land of Sinai,"* exhorting fighters and wannabe recruits to go forth.

The Islamic State also has highlighted how it has scuttled gas deals, killed spies and built a foundation for tawhid (*pure monotheism*). Most recently, it released an ideological video, but it was not a stern lecture like those posted by al-Qaeda-styled groups. The video showed individuals in Wilayat Sinai hanging out together around a campfire, showing the life of a mujahid and the camaraderie involved, imbuing a particular ascetic for future members who join up.

Moving west, the Islamic State's activities and operations are even more sophisticated and closer to how it operates in Syria and Iraq, though on a smaller scale. Libya has the most potential to replicate the Islamic State's model in Mesopotamia if things go right for it.

Majlis Shura Shabab al-Islam, based in Derna and the named used prior to the Islamic State's formal acceptance of its baya, was already involved in a variety of military, governance and dawa activities. Though in reality it only truly controls some neighborhoods in Derna, the activities have only increased and the Islamic State now also operates in Benghazi, Sirte, and Tripoli, and has created the self-styled Wilayat al-Barqah in the east, Wilayat al-Tarabulus in the west, and Wilayat al-Fizan in the south.

There are also some signs that the Islamic State has siphoned off some of Ansar al-Sharia in Libya's members, which could help accelerate its rise similar to how the Islamic State absorbed defecting Jabhat al-Nusra members in Syria.

Beyond the military fighting the Islamic State is doing in Derna and Benghazi, as well as its military parades in Sirte and an attack in Wilayat al-Fizan, it has also claimed to have executed two Tunisian journalists (*though this has since been disputed by Tunisia's ambassador in Libya*), kidnapped 21 Christian Egyptians, and conducted an attack on the Corinthia Hotel in Tripoli.

In terms of governance types of activities, the Islamic State in Libya has primarily only focused on cultural symbolism. For example, it has conducted a number of hisbah (*accountability*) patrols in markets in Derna and Sirte making sure they are sharia-compliant and are not selling rotten or spoiled food, taking away stores selling hookahs since they view smoking tobacco as against Islam, and telling stores to stop selling their products when it is time for daily prayers.

The Islamic State in Libya has also conducted some dawa activities, the largest was the forum *"The Caliphate Upon the Manhaj [methodology] of the Prophet"*. It has also provided aid to the poor and needy and given gifts and sweets to children in Benghazi. The Islamic State now is attempting to impose regulations on locals within the health industry, specifically those in pharmacies.

On top of this, unlike the other wilayat there are clear signs that there is a foreign fighter presence in Libya. This is not to the same extent as in Syria or Iraq, but the fact that there are foreigners there illustrates the theaters appeal. Although the Islamic State's official presence in Libya did not begin until November 2013, jihadi foreign fighters have been coming into Libya since 2012 when Algerians from al-Qaeda in the Islamic Maghreb began to make it another base of operations and a safe haven.

There have also been a number of foreigners that have been members of Ansar al-Sharia in Libya in part due to the relationship and connections with its sister organization in Tunisia as well as its training for individuals to go fight abroad in Syria.

Most confirmed foreign fighters have come from surrounding countries to Libya, such as Morocco, Algeria, Tunisia, Egypt and Sudan. Though there have also been cases of Saudi and Yemeni foreign fighters, as well as rumors of Palestinians and Syrians. It is difficult to know the total number of foreign fighters since some have left for other fights in Syria or the Sinai after receiving training or returned home to carry out attacks in Egypt or Tunisia. It is believed though that Tunisians make up the highest percentage of foreign fighters in Libya and that up to 20 percent of the jihadi fighters in Libya are of foreign origin.

Another sign of the importance and emphasis the Islamic State is placing on foreign fighter involvement in Libya is that its official media apparatus is beginning to announce martyrdom notices, as it has done in Iraq and Syria. Since it began, it has announced 10 cases, including six Tunisians, two

Egyptians, one Saudi and one Sudanese all who died in the battles of Benghazi. Further, to encourage more emigration, the Islamic State released a story about how one Saudi fighter, Abd al-Hamid al-Qasimi, traveled to Libya to embark on the building of the "caliphate" in Wilayat Tarabulus.

More importantly, and in line with the Islamic State's media methodologies in Mesopotamia, it released a video message from two ethnic-Tuareg members of the Islamic State in Wilayat Tarbulus calling for individuals and jihadis in Azawad (*a term used by some locals as a name for northern Mali*) to pledge baya to Baghdadi and make hijrah (*emigration*) to the Islamic State in Libya.

One of the men, Abu Umar al-Tawrigi, stated: "*I call my Tuareg brothers to migrate to the Islamic State and that they give baya to emir al-muminin [leader of the faithful] Abu Bakr Al- Baghdadi.*" Dozens of similar videos have come from the Islamic State's foreign fighters based in Syria, from Bosnians to Canadians to French to Indonesians to Moldovans, among others that have produced videos in a similar vein.

The Islamic State does therefore seem to be attempting to follow the same tactics and strategies on the ground in Libya (*and to a lesser extent in the Sinai*) as it has already done in Iraq and Syria. There is still a long way to go before either is consolidated in terms of territorial control or full monopoly on governance and security. Libya has the highest likelihood of success since there is no state, though there are limitations too since there is a multi-polar devolution of a variety of armed actors.

The Islamic State will likely have more problems in the Sinai since the actors are stuck between two strong military states in Egypt and Israel as well as a Hamas-led Gaza government that fears the jihadis' threat to its legitimacy. That said, if the Egyptian government continues to operate in a brazen manner militarily it will create new local recruits that could sustain the Islamic State in north Sinai. How this all ends is impossible to predict, but as of now, the Islamic State has indeed set itself up on a limited base in the Sinai and has established a growing movement in Libya more than two months following the announcement of its expansion.

The Ambitions of the 'Islamic State'

By now, many have seen the variations of maps that "Islamic State" (IS) activists have posted online showing aspirational future areas of conquest. This genre usually encompasses areas that have been under historical Caliphates shaded in black, including places such as Spain or Greece that do not even have a Muslim plurality of the population today. Ultimately, IS (*as well as other Sunni jihadi groups*) hopes the entire world comes under its dominion. This is nothing new.

All of this, is of course, contingent on any level of success and legitimacy, which at this juncture will be difficult in the face of most Muslims rejecting its "Caliphate" announcement as well other Islamist groups including pro-al-Qaeda jihadis.

The "Caliphate project" is a unique enterprise and one that does not necessarily play by the same rules most follow, since ultimately its goal is to overthrow the Westphalian nation-state model and the post-World War II American international system. The announcement of the renewed "Caliphate" could signal something more akin to a colonial project where the "Islamic state" seeks to incorporate non-contiguous territories. Already in Iraq and Syria, the areas it has taken control of are not all contiguous. Therefore, it is plausible that factions or groups in other locales could conceivably take territory and, having pledged bay'a (*an oath of loyalty*) to the Islamic State's self-proclaimed Caliph Abu Bakr al-Baghdadi, thereby expanding the State's Caliphate.

Unlike al-Qaeda, which has mainly used its foreign fighter contingents to train, plan, and then execute attacks in the West or Arab countries over the years, IS might have bigger plans for them. While IS would have no problem with dispatching foreign fighters for terrorist attacks out of theater (*more on this below*), they might also order their foreign fighter cadres to build up capacities for the expansion of its state once they return home. Further, it may also use them to infiltrate and subvert al-Qaeda branches and cells as part of its broader war with al-Qaeda for supremacy over the global jihadi movement.

The Islamic State's colonial Caliphate project would find the most fertile ground in the Northern Sinai, Eastern Libya, and some of the neighborhoods in poor areas of Western European cities that are Muslim-majority. None of this is inevitable. In fact, the Islamic State would have some serious difficulties in pulling it off, especially in Western Europe. But the jihadi movement has never let feasibility stand in the way of its ambitions. Like many jihadi strategists have proposed in the past, they would hope to set off a backlash that could lead to destabilization and chaos. This is exactly what jihadis thrive off. We have already seen failed attempts in England to establish "sharia zones" by local jihadis like the UK-based Anjem Choudary, who has cautiously spoken out in favor of the Caliphate claim.

Besides the Islamic State's ideological and narrative appeal, one of the biggest sources of its strength comes from its economic independence. Due to the spoils of war and criminal enterprises, they are far less reliant on private donors than al-Qaeda. Unlike al-Qaeda, the Islamic State has funding and can use its extra coffers to offer money to potential affiliates. It is a new center that can give resources to the periphery. In recent years, al-Qaeda has had more difficulty doing that.

The Islamic State's economic independence is also germane because many foreign fighters have criminal pasts and therefore would have experiences and have no issue with getting involved in criminal activities if and when they return home. Additionally, those outside the center of the Islamic State's gravity can leverage the criminal networks in locales like the Sinai and Libya. There has already been signs that jihadis have attempted to graft onto those criminal networks with varying success.

Similarly, one could see a scenario where Europe's foreign fighters — many of whom have deep criminal pasts — return home and set up business rackets and other illegal ventures in certain neighborhoods in areas where they are from and run them like mafia bosses or gangsters. This could lead to a chilling effect such as no-go zones where European police are not comfortable entering or operating.

Again, this is all hypothetical and not the current reality, but setting up such independent economic hubs in "statelets" could further the reach of the Islamic State, which has no time frame on its project. The success of such an undertaking would likely have an easier chance of working in the Sinai/Libya scenario due to lack of full state writ already.

Following the announcement of the Islamic State's self-proclaimed Caliphate, its leader Abu Bakr al-Baghdadi delivered a Ramadan address, which was filled with the usual jihadi platitudes. It also included specific "shout outs" to areas where Muslims are suffering and could be a clue to areas it hopes to expand its influence or compete with al-Qaeda.

For instance, Baghdadi specifically notes the suffering of Sunnis in Burma, the Philippines, Indonesia, Kashmir, Bosnia, the Caucasus, Palestine, Egypt, East Turkistan (China), Iran, France, Tunisia, and Central African Republic. There is already known public support for the Islamic State or has foreign fighter networks that have fed itself in Iraq and Syria in the Philippines, Indonesia, Bosnia, the Caucasus, Palestine, Egypt, Iran, France, and Tunisia. Therefore, if one wants to look to areas that are not in surrounding countries to Iraq or Syria these are potentially more immediate targets.

Closer to home, though, the Islamic State hopes to expand its reach in terms of linking up contiguous territory over "Sykes-Picot" borders. More recently, for the first time publicly the Islamic State has announced a presence in the Qalamoun region on the Lebanese-Syrian border as well as claiming responsibility for an attack in Beirut.

If it hopes to expand into Lebanon, it will have to compete with the Qaeda-aligned Abdullah Azzam Brigades, which has years of experience recruiting. Similarly, while there has been support in Ma'an, Jordan for the Islamic State, this is a minority sentiment in the broader Jordanian jihadi current, which has been closer to and more supportive of Jabhat al-Nusra in Syria.

The biggest prize beyond targeting Israel would be provoking violence against the Saudi regime and claiming Saudi territory. The majority of the 1,400+ Saudis that have gone to fight in Syria (*and now Iraq*) have joined the Islamic State rather than Jabhat al-Nusra. Additionally, hundreds in the last decade fought with the group when it was called al-Qaeda in Iraq. Among them, some then went onto fight with al-Qaeda in the Arabian Peninsula (AQAP). There are also number of its foreign fighters that have returned home and other soft support inside the Kingdom.

Therefore, it is possible that the Islamic State may rely on those already inside Saudi, Yemen, and its own soldiers in Iraq to create a three-pronged attack. While the Saudi government would have air superiority, it has no significant experience in quelling an insurgency (though Saudi has been successful in counterterrorism campaigns against al-Qaeda) and could prove more difficult if it was drawn out. This in of itself would be a win for the Islamic State, "remaining" sometimes is just as important as outright victory.

The biggest win for the Islamic State though would be becoming a real player in the Israeli-Palestinian fight. This would be easier said than done and would rely on a number of factors falling into place. In the past, the global jihadi movement in Palestine was more aspirational than a true force on the ground. In the aftermath of the Arab uprisings and with space filled by the movement in northern Sinai global jihadis have been able to make in-roads, albeit still a relatively small movement. Domestically, the continued failed governance of Hamas in Gaza and continued corruption and general illegitimacy that Fatah has as a result of perceived collaboration with Israel in the West Bank has also been helpful.

What could propel the Islamic State in the Palestinian arena is another Intifada. In light of the above wariness and failures by the status quo Palestinian political parties, there has been a rise in Salafism in both Gaza and the West Bank. Therefore, similar to Hamas' rise in the aftermath of both the first and second intifadas, it is possible that the consequence of a third intifada would be that the Islamic State would be able to carve a space out for itself, especially if it is perceived as the underdog punching above its weight and giving blows to the hated "Zionists."

If this came to fruition, it is possible that because the Islamic State is fighting Israel, it would lower the bar for support of the Islamic State due to a legitimate, but, at times, irrationally visceral hatred for Israel even if the group that is fighting this "resistance" or "jihad" against Israel has authoritarian tendencies, too. As a result, it is the hope of the Islamic State in the medium to longer-term that if it wins the Palestinians, it will subsequently then win the Muslim world.

Another way the Islamic State could gain "ungoverned" spaces or build up its capacities and networks is through creating breakaway groups of members that defect from al-Qaeda branches to new Islamic State "territories" in places like Syria, Yemen, Somalia, or North Africa. The recent successes on the battlefield in Iraq (*and now again in Syria due to a shifting of new resources gained in the Iraqi offensive*) and the announcement of the Caliphate, the Islamic State perceives that this could push more factions, individuals, or groups to join up with its cause and reject the "out of touch" leader of al-Qaeda Ayman al-Zawahiri.

Recently, in light of these Iraqi offensives, whether it is legitimate or through coercion, members and leaders within Jabhat al-Nusra in both the Deir al-Zour and Damascus region have defected, pledged bay'a to Baghdadi, and joined the Islamic State. There are also unconfirmed rumors that foot soldiers in both AQAP and Harakat al-Shabab al-Mujahidin, al-Qaeda's Somali branch, have some sympathies for the Islamic State. Thus far, we have already seen al-Qaeda in the Islamic Maghreb's Central Region officially splitting and supporting the Islamic State.

We have also seen some members and a leader in AQAP that went to Syria to fight that have since backed the Islamic State, too. All of those pledges of fealty occurred prior to the Islamic State's Caliphate announcement. Since then, the only relevant bay'a given was by a faction from within the Tehrik-i-Taliban Pakistan, a group known for its close ties to al-Qaeda, which itself had nine members defect to Baghdadi.

The Islamic State hopes this trend continues. The biggest potential tipping point would be for AQAP to switch sides since it is still rightly perceived as al-

Qaeda's strongest branch. While AQAP's senior leadership has loyalty to Zawahiri and al-Qaeda, in part because of its leader, Nasir al-Wihayshi's mentorship under Usama bin Ladin in Afghanistan.

One thing to look for going forward is whether the large Saudi contingent that fought with the Islamic State in Iraq and Syria and then returns to Yemen to continue jihad with AQAP decides to make a power play against AQAP's senior leadership or attempts to fracture the organization and create a breakaway group while also taking members from AQAP with it.

One way that the Islamic State hopes any of these various potentialities comes to fruition is that it compels the West to focus more on its own homelands instead of security in the broader Arab world. This could be done through dispatching any number of the up to thousands of Westerners in its ranks to conduct terrorist attacks in the West. Thereby, creating a distraction for Western countries, while the Islamic State is continuing its hoped takeover of more territory and resources in the region.

As a result, it is a misnomer to think that it is an either/or policy for the Islamic State to only be interested in just state-building or terrorism. As we have seen with AQAP in the past, the Islamic State will likely be in the business of both. For this potential plan to work out, though, the Islamic State will need to expand its support base beyond just its most hardcore following and address some of the skepticism and issues that top jihadi scholars like Shaykh Abu Muhammad al-Maqdisi have warned it about. Otherwise, all these aspirational ambitions will be for naught.

The Islamic State's Archipelago of Provinces

This week, Abu Bakr al-Baghdadi, the leader of the Islamic State of Iraq and al-Sham, released a rare public message in which he declared the creation of several new "provinces" in various Arab countries. It was the first time that he and his organization have acknowledged groups that have pledged *baya* (religiously binding oath of allegiance) to the so-called "Islamic State" since the announcement of its "Caliphate" six months ago. The audio message offers insight into the group's expansion model and its plans for exacerbating religious tensions between Sunnis and Shiites beyond Iraq, Syria, and Lebanon. Whether Western governments want to admit it or not, the reality is that the Islamic State has expanded in a non-contiguous manner outside its base and now has authority over satellite groups and small amounts of territory outside Iraq and the Levant.

Since the caliphate announcement in June, a cacophony of different individuals and groups have pledged *baya* to Baghdadi. Yet in this week's audio message, he only recognized the annexation of jihadist elements in Saudi Arabia and Yemen, along with jihadist groups in Algeria (Jund al-Khilafah), Libya (Majlis Shura Shabab al-Islam), and Sinai (Ansar Beit al-Maqdis). He ignored non-Arab factions based in Pakistan, Indonesia, the Philippines, and elsewhere that have made similar pledges to him. This could suggest tighter links with fellow Arab jihadists, or that the organizations outside the Arab world are not ready for exploitation and growth.

Baghdadi also noted that his declaration entails "nullification" of the local groups in the five places mentioned above, as well as "the announcement of new *wilayat* (provinces) of the Islamic State and the appointment of *wulat* (governors) for them." While he claimed to annex these "territories," publicly available information indicates that only the groups in Libya and Sinai can legitimately claim to control land -- the validity of such claims in Saudi Arabia, Yemen, and Algeria remains to be seen.

That said, those groups that do have proven territorial control -- which are now being dubbed Wilayat Libya and Wilayat Sinai -- could follow the same economic model of sustainability that the Islamic State has pursed in Iraq and Syria over the past couple years. If they have not done so already, the Libyan and Sinai groups are prime candidates for fully grafting their jihadist networks onto the traditional criminal enterprise networks that have been used for trafficking, smuggling, and other black market activities over the years. Therefore, these two new "provinces" could have some level of viability, at least in the short term. Questions remain about whether this model can be employed by the Islamic State's new Algerian, Saudi, and Yemeni members, who do not seem to control any territory at this juncture.

In addition to declaring the annexations, Baghdadi made clear to his associates in Saudi Arabia and Yemen that it is time to start an overt military campaign against the *rafidah*, a derogatory term for Shiites that literally means "rejectionists." He also emphasized the order of priority, stating that jihadists in Wilayat al-Haramayn ("The Province of the Two Holy Places," meaning Saudi Arabia) and Wilayat Yemen should first target Shiites (including the Houthis), then the Saudi dynasty, and then finally the "Crusaders." In doing so, he formally clarified how the Islamic State perceives its enemies and its most immediate threat, while also illustrating its differences from al-Qaeda, an organization that has historically given precedent to fighting the "Crusaders" first.

If the Islamic State's followers in Saudi Arabia or Yemen follow through on this call for a campaign against Shiites, outsiders will be better able to measure the group's true influence and its level of command and control over those outside its base territory. Whatever happens, Baghdadi's message highlights his desire to continue projecting power in new areas. The Islamic State is staying true to its slogan of "remaining and expanding," in part to show the anti-ISIS coalition that while it may not have the same battlefield momentum it had this summer, it is still controlling territory in Iraq and Syria. For the group's leaders and adherents, this is a victory in of itself, supposedly highlighting how the will of God is on their side even as the world is against them.

In the end, the Islamic State's ability to expand its reach and its writ will depend on how successful this now-formalized annexation model proves to be. For now, and perhaps for the long term, this means the U.S.-led coalition will have to deal with a more complex threat environment.

Islamic State Secures New Haven in Libya

Two rival governments in Libya have fought an increasingly bloody civil war since last summer, as the world paid little attention. While they battled for control of the country's oil wealth, a third force—Islamic State—took advantage of the chaos to grow stronger. The beheading of 21 Egyptian Christians by Islamic State followers has finally drawn the global spotlight to the group's rising clout in Libya, which not long ago was touted as a successful example of Western intervention. The killings prompted Egyptian airstrikes on Islamic State strongholds in Libya and spurred calls for more active international involvement in what is fast becoming a failed state on Europe's doorstep.

The Libyan affiliate of Islamic State in Syria and Iraq has, in fact, been spreading its sway for months. First it established an area of control last fall in and around the eastern city of Derna, a historical center of Libyan jihadists. Recently, it also took over parts of former dictator Moammar Gadhafi's hometown of Sirte, on the central coast, setting up a radio station there and sending Islamic morality patrols onto the streets

All the while, the two rival governments of Libya focused on combatting one another, each supported by regional powers. Both preferred to largely ignore the influx of foreign jihadists forming new alliances with local extremists—and their unification under Islamic State's banner.

Libya isn't the only place outside Syria and Iraq where the extremist group has established affiliates, largely by absorbing homegrown jihadist groups into its project of world domination and religious war until the total triumph of Islam. There are also Islamic State "provinces" in Egypt's Sinai Peninsula, in Yemen, and in so-called Khorasan, a region straddling Afghanistan and Pakistan.

Islamic State's slickly produced video of the slaughter of the Egyptian Copts, concluded with the promise to conquer Rome, the historic center of Christendom. That threat is bound to reinforce existing pressure in countries such as France and Italy for a military intervention to stave off the complete collapse of Libya, which is just across the Mediterranean Sea from Italy.

"*The situation in Libya has been out of control for three years*," Italy's Prime Minister Matteo Renzi cautioned in a television interview after the video's release. "*We shouldn't go from total indifference to hysteria.*" Libya has been unstable since Gadhafi's ouster and killing in 2011, but it descended into all-out civil war last summer.

One side is the old parliament, elected in 2012 and dominated by the Muslim Brotherhood and its allies. It includes militias from the conservative city of Misrata, a key force in the revolution against the Gadhafi regime. That parliament, known as the General National Congress, was replaced in last elections by another legislature, the House of Representatives, dominated by more secular and nationalist forces.

While the international community has recognized the new House of Representatives as the legitimate new authority in Libya, the GNC refused to accept its electoral defeat. Militias affiliated with the GNC drove the new administration out of Tripoli to the eastern city of Tobruk, triggering what soon became an all-out war that destroyed the Tripoli airport and valuable oil infrastructure.

As the West was distracted by Islamic State's blitz through Syria and Iraq last year, regional powers unleashed a proxy war in Libya. Egypt's President Abdel Fattah Al Sisi, who ousted the Muslim Brotherhood from power in his own country in 2013, threw his weight behind the Tobruk government, arming and assisting it. So did Egypt's regional allies, Saudi Arabia and United Arab Emirates.

Meanwhile, Turkey and Qatar - supporters of Islamist causes around the region - rallied behind Tripoli, as did Sudan. By then, however, it may have already been too late to stop Islamic State's spread, especially as the Tripoli administration has long played down the threat posed by Islamist militants.

Islamic State attacked the Corinthia Hotel in Tripoli, killing several foreigners and showcasing its ability to operate in the heart of the capital. Amazingly, the Tripoli administration's reaction to that outrage was to allege that the massacre was a provocation carried out by its Tobruk rivals and Egypt. Since then, most of the last Westerners in town left Tripoli.

The latest Islamic State attack, on the Coptic Egyptians, was intended to directly draw Egypt into the Libyan conflict, said Khalil al-Anani, an Egyptian scholar of Islamist movements at Johns Hopkins University. Mr. Sisi, whose takeover in 2013 was widely popular among Egypt's Coptic minority, has positioned himself as a defender of the country's Christians; He became the first Egyptian president to visit a Coptic church on Christmas.

But his task of thwarting Islamic State grows more complicated. His army already faces a deadly Islamic State insurgency in the eastern Sinai Peninsula, losing hundreds of soldiers over the past two years.

The Rise and Decline of Ansar al-Sharia

Over the past two years, global attention has shifted to Syria and Iraq with the rise of Jabhat al-Nusra and the return of the Islamic State of Iraq and al-Sham (ISIS). However, nearly one thousand miles to the west, Ansar al-Sharia in Libya (ASL) has continued its work of facilitating a future Islamic state since the spectacular attack on the American consulate in Benghazi on September 11, 2012.

Initially, ASL launched a highly sophisticated program of dawa (*outreach*) which included the provisioning of social services both inside and outside of Libya. This has provided it with an avenue for local support. But since Libyan General Khalifa Haftar announced a major offensive against Islamist armed groups in eastern Libya in May 2014 (*codenamed Operation Dignity*), ASL has focused primarily on military action.

ASL's fortunes have dropped dramatically in the process, further exacerbated by the death of its leader, Muhammad al-Zahawi, confirmed in January 2015, and ISIS' intensification of its efforts to create a Libyan base independent of ASL since November 2014.

In many ways, ASL followed the model of Ansar al-Sharia in Tunisia (AST), viewing its outreach and social services campaign as an important part of establishing and building not only an Islamic society, but an eventual Islamic state governed by its interpretations of Sharia (Islamic law). In contrast to the Libyan government, which is often corrupt, incompetent, or extractive, ASL worked to convince the local population of its own competence and benevolence. Critically, this helped it win greater public support.

In addition to ASL's reach across Libya, from Benghazi, Tripoli and Ajdabiya to Sirte, Darna and the Gulf of Sidra, among other smaller locales, it has also operated abroad. Most notably, it has dispatched operatives to Syria, Sudan and Gaza to assist in humanitarian relief efforts. This has added a whole new layer to the meaning of global jihad and how various groups might try to engage populations outside their local areas of operation.

ASL has enjoyed a number of identities as an organization: On the one hand, it has been a charity, a security service, a health service and areligious education provider; on the other hand, it is also a militia, a terrorist organization and a training base for foreign jihadists. In recognition of this complexity, this analysis looks at the full spectrum ofthe group and teases out ASL's dawa campaign locally and globally; its hopes and future plans based off of its dawa literature on aqida (creed) and manhaj (methodology); its training of foreign fighters for the

Syrian conflict as well as for the conflict with General Haftar; and, the rise of ISIS as a competitor.

In the aftermath of the Arab uprisings, most specifically in countries like Egypt, Libya and Tunisia where regimes were fully overthrown, the public sphere opened. These countries also represented a fresh start and laboratory for a new jihadi campaign in the wake of al-Qaeda in Iraq's (AQI) failures at controlling territory and instituting governance last decade.

For example, al-Qaeda leader Ayman al-Zawahiri thought that this new environment provided an opportunity *"for dawa and informing...Only God knows for how long they [local governments and the West] will continue, so the people of Islam and Jihad should benefit from them and exploit them."* In the same audio message, he further emphasized the superiority of Sharia over all other legal systems and laws. Zawahiri also endorsed the liberation of Islamic lands, opposed normalizing relations with Israel and underscored the importance of "cleansing thelands" of financial and social corruption.

In 2004, the foremost respected Sunni jihadi ideologue alive today, Abu Muhammad al-Maqdisi, wrote Waqafat ma' Thamrat al-Jihad (*Stances on the Fruit of Jihad*) in an attempt to steer the jihadi movement away from the abuses of his former student and AQI leader, Abu Musab al-Zarqawi.

In the book, Maqdisi examines the differences between what he describes as qital al- nikayya (*fighting to hurt or damage the enemy*) and qital al-tamkin (*fighting to consolidate one's power*). Maqdisi argues that the former provides only short-term tactical victories whereas the latter provides a framework for consolidating an Islamic state. Implicit is Maqdisi's emphasis on the importance of planning, organization, education and dawa.

The formation of ASL along with its sister organizations in Tunisia (AST) and Egypt (ASE) were seen as logical conclusions and implementations of Zawahiri's and Maqdisi's ideas. In short, these groups selected a dawa-first strategy instead of a jihad-first strategy. As a result, one of the main avenues through which ASL advanced its ideas was its social services programs. This cultivation of followers in a broad fashion – in contrast to the more vanguard-oriented organizations that have been involved in jihadism in a local, regional, or global capacity over the past 30 years – was seen as a new way to consolidate a future Islamic state.

At first, this approach appeared to forge a new and successful way forward for the jihadi movement, with an unprecedented number of individuals joining ASL and AST. Over the past two years, however, this dawa-first approached has backfired. Within a month of Abdel Fattah el-Sisi's coup d'état in Egypt in early July 2013, all of the key members of ASE had either been arrested or had been forced to link-up with Jama'at Ansar Bayt al-Maqdis' growing insurgency in northern Sinai. Still others had fled to Syria to join the jihad against the Bashar al-Assad regime.

Less than two months later, at the end of August 2013, the Tunisian government designated AST as a terrorist organization and proceeded to dismantle it via widespread arrests. As a result, some Tunisians left for Libya and joined up with ASL while others went to Syria and joined ISIS.

As for ASL, once General Haftar launched his war against them, it too mostly stopped conducting regular dawa. The dawa events it did sponsor were publicized after the fact and related to providing meat and food to the poor and needy during Ramadan, Eid al-Fitr and Eid al-Adha in the summer and fall of 2014.

Instead, much of what has been published by ASL since then has been related to the fighting with General Haftar's forces. Additionally, while still boasting of members in other cities, ASL has confined the vast majority of its military operations to Benghazi. And while ASL has not disintegrated like ASE or AST, its capacities have been severely degraded, providing ISIS with an opening in the fall of 2014.

At the height of ASL's campaign, it oversaw an extensive network of services inside and outside of Libya. In fact, it was involved in activities ranging from anti-drug campaigns, blood drives and food drives (including the slaughtering of animals on holidays for the poor) to Quranic competitions for children, housing projects for the poor, school cleanings, garbage removals and bridge repairs.

ASL provided such tangible services to the community as opening a medical clinic for women and children, an Islamic Center for Women, an Emergency Room and a religious school named Mirkaz al-Imam al-Bukhari Li- l-'Ulum al-Sharia. ASL also maintained security at the major al-Jala'hospital in Benghazi.

What made these efforts much more impressive was that ASL was not just acting independently, but was getting support and co-sponsorship from other local organizations. The blood drives were coordinated with the Benghazi Central Blood Center (CBC), for which the CBC even presented ASL with an award on July 25, 2013. ASL also coordinated lectures with the Social Security Fund's Benghazi Branch and cleaned roads in cooperation with the electrical company and Tajama' al-Qawarshah al-Khayri wa-l-Da'wai.

Moreover, the most successful program that ASL undertook was a vigorous anti-drug campaign together with the Rehab Clinic at the Psychiatric Hospital of Benghazi, the Ahli Club (soccer), Libya Company (Telecom and Technology) and the Technical Company. While in Sirte, ASL hosted a ten-day Quranic competition during Ramadan in association with the Office of Awqaf of Sirte, Radio Tawhid of Sirte, the Cleaning Services Company and the University of Sirte. Also during Ramadan, ASL assisted in a food drive that gained sponsorship from the Libya Company, Primera Gallery, al-Iman Foundation, Tajama' al-Qawarshah al-Khayri wa-l-Da'wai and the Faruq Center.

Beyond its local efforts, ASL launched a robust campaign abroad too, targeting Syria, Sudan and Gaza. ASL dubbed these overseas dawa efforts *"The Convoy Campaign of Goodness To Our People in 'X-location.'"* These efforts began in November 2012 when ASL sent aid packages to Syria and Gaza, including its dawa literature. The most sophisticated operation, however, came in response to the major flooding that hit Sudan in August 2013. An ASL team landed in Khartoum with five tons of medicine, twelves tons of grains and legumes and eight tons of children's milk in tow. The second delivery contained twenty-four tons of clothing and 1.5 tons of floor carpets for mosques. All of these items and packages were stamped or plastered with ASL's logo.

The level of aid in itself was outstanding, but the fact that it came from a global jihadi organization that had procured and delivered it safely to Sudan's capital testifies to the group's organizational capabilities as well as its possible ties to the Sudanese government.

The same types of questions apply to ASL's operations in Syria, and its potential ties to the Turkish state. In Syria, the campaign was called *"Uplifting the Ummah, freedom from forced rule, Western dominance, and uplifted by the goodness, pride and dignity under the law of Rahman (one of the holiest of the 99 names of God within Islam)."*

In late January 2014, ASL sent three tranches of aid, comprising slaughtered beef, flour and electric generators, to the rural Latakia towns of Salma and Kasab, among others. The effort in Syria illustrated a high level of planning and organization, since ASL had to gain access to local resources and grasp the human topography of the area. Lastly, also in late January 2014, ASL responded to an Israeli airstrike in Gaza.

The campaign was marketed as *"We are over here in Libya and our eyes are on Jerusalem."* ASL's contacts inside Gaza went door-to-door in the al-Nafaq neighborhood distributing cash-filled envelopes with ASL's logo to those "*whose houses were damaged by the shelling of the Zionists.*" The speed of the campaign suggests the possibility of an ASL network in Gaza.

While impressive, these overseas campaigns represent the height of ASL's influence and power. Since the fighting with General Haftar has commenced, ASL has shown no signs of continuing its international campaign. Instead, it has shifted increasingly into self-preservation mode. Prior to discussing the war with General Haftar, however, it is important to highlight the ideological backbone of ASL, especially since its key points are part of the literature that ASL had distributed during its local and international dawa.

One of the most important pamphlets that ASL passed out during its dawa efforts educated individuals on its doctrine and agenda. ASL's core ideology has particular global jihadi underpinnings. First, there is immense emphasis on the tawhid (pure monotheism) of God, as "*there is no other God, and there is nothing that can be revered like Him.*" The source of "interference or deduction" is the Quran, the "word of God Almighty," and the Sunna (*actions and sayings of the Prophet Muhammad*), which "sets out and explains the Quran."

Second, as the pamphlet makes clear, if a Muslim does not follow the literal authority of God, then he is branded or "excommunicated" as a kafir (unbeliever). Anyone who "*calls for anything other than Islam,*" such as "democracy" or "secularism," manifests infidelity, or kufr, and is deemed "nugatory." The permissibility of takfir (excommunication) appears to stem from the institutional necessity to impose obedience through a set of actions and beliefs extracted and interpreted literally from the Quran and the Sunna.

Third, the pamphlet maintains that the theological mechanism to purget he Ummah (Islamic community) of kufr and to implement tawhid is military jihad. Jihad does not require a religious verdict set down by an imam because fighting the kufar (infidels) is "more obligatory in the world than adhering to the [Islamic] faith." Thus, waging jihad is considered a fundamental prerequisite to being considered a genuine Muslim.

If a Muslim wages jihad against the declared kufar, then ASL will not "accuse [that Muslim] of being a sinner."

Moreover, the "blood of Muslims is not haram," or forbidden, because there is no higher duty than jihad. The prioritization of military strength and discipline is the sine qua non of uniting the Ummah into one Muslim entity. Political parties, even Islamic ones, represent a pluralistic, democratic process, and therefore serve to "divide up the Ummah."

Ultimately, ASL aims to establish an authoritative, theological state based on Sharia to supplant the current laws and constitution. ASL's agenda appears to be local; namely, to fight rival militias in a war tocontrol Libya and to reform it into an Islamic state. However, the beliefs and theological justifications for violent action suggest a complete rejection of the current world order and constant conflict.

Another of ASL's pamphlets explains its issues with democracy in detail. Besides its focus on tawhid and the necessity of jihad, ASL has a deep aversion to democracy. The pamphlet's main argument is that "democracy" constitutes the antithesis to shura (council), or Islamic governance based on Sharia. There are three fundamental differences that make democracy and Islam incompatible: democracy is based on the "rule of the people" while shura is based on the "rule of God"; democracy enforces man-made laws forbidden in Islam while shura uses judicial ijtihad (independent reasoning) to make individual evaluations of cases in strict accordance with Islamic teachings; and, democratic systems are ruled by people while shura is ruled by God.

The purpose of the pamphlet is to delegitimize those Arab leaders who claim to be pious Muslims but govern and acquire political power through, or under the guise of, democracy. More importantly, by placing democracy and Islam in irreconcilable positions, ASL undercuts Islamic democratic parties, such as the Libyan Muslim Brotherhood's Justice and Construction Party, which seek to apply Islamic principles to public policy within a democratic framework.

For ASL, not only is "democracy" fundamentally incompatible with Islam, but it is also framed in its literature as an authoritarian system.

As the pamphlet makes clear, ASL directly associates the offshoots of liberal values found in many democratic societies, such as "lusts," "defamation" and "wine, clown-like behavior, songs, debaucherous behavior, adultery [and] cinemas" with the imposition of kufr institutions such as the Charter of the United Nations, the laws of the General Assembly and the "laws of [democratically-elected] parties."

Thus, the logic follows: if one does not engage in acts of lust and defamation, then one is deemed "extreme, terroristic and not tending towards world peace and coexistence." By imposing specific non-Islamic values on society and excluding Sharia-sanctioned law, "democracy" directly seeks to eradicate Islam. Moreover, elected assemblies and parliaments are built by "majority rule," a concept that "bears no relation to the Quran and the Hadith," and thus seeks to eradicate God-sanctioned rule. Lastly, ASL tars democracy with the failure of the Arab uprisings to bring about better governance, especially in Egypt,

Tunisia, Jordan and Yemen. The lesson learned from those uprisings is that democracy is full of "provisions and deceitful illusions." Essentially, the pre-Arab uprising dictators and civil unrest that followed are the products of "democracy."

A third pamphlet that ASL has distributed among its supporters and would-be recruits is on how to handle interactions with police officers, should they be stopped in the street. This pamphlet provides talking points relating to the current Libyan system in order to sow doubts among the police and encourage defections.

ASL talking points include invoking God as one and the only arbitrator and source of governing authority, while the role of humans is emphasized as simply fighting" whatever governs that does not come from God." God, the ASL pamphlet argues, "will not rely on [humans] for governing," but simply to eradicate "evil" or anything that does not adhere to a literal interpretation of Islamic texts. By prosecuting criminals under Libyan civil code, policemen are actually "forcing people into kufr" because those people become subject to taghut (tyrants). The concepts of "policemen" and the "army" are not rejected, but only if the authorities "legislate" with Sharia.

A final ideological statement worth highlighting pertains to ASL's global outlook. While ASL has focused mainly on local issues, it does have a global dimension and is very much within the ideological milieu of global jihadism. ASL's statement in response to the United States' seizure of Abu Anas al-Libi, a Libyan wanted for his part in the 1998

East Africa embassy bombings, is emblematic of its global outlook. Ultimately, ASL argues that the United States is seeking to destroy Islam and impose its own culture, values and laws on Muslims and their lands. The U.S., called al-kufar, does this in three ways. First, it is "preventing the Muslims from establishing an [Islamic] state." Examples of this are coalition campaigns against the Taliban in Afghanistan and Islamists in northern Mali.

Second, the statement charges that the "war against and pursuit of jihad and the mujahideen," or "war against terrorism," is "at its essence a war against Islam." When intervening in other countries' affairs, the U.S. often targets "whoever they wish unsupervised and unaccountable" (an allusion to al-Libi, but more importantly the killing of Osama bin Laden without Pakistani consultation) while "violating holy sites and [Muslim]lands" (an allusion to Operation Desert Shield, Iraqi Freedom). Under the pretext of fighting terrorism, the U.S. as the "decision-maker and leader of the world" is in reality attempting to impose its "unlawful assertions of 'superiority' over creation." ASL attributes Libya's chaos to the U.S. intervention and subsequent attempt to impose the "tyranny of democracy," which is fully preventing the rule of Sharia. This aggression, arrogance and lack of respect for Muslims derives from the United States' kafir values of "murder and displacement" – a clear reference to America's history of slavery, troubled race relations and conflicts with Native Americans.

Third, ASL argues that "terrorism" is used by the U.S. as a label for those who do not adhere to their "democratic" agenda. In response, ASL calls for a mass campaign to "inform every Muslim of the goals of these belligerent states and their allies." The logic is that before being able and willing to wage jihad, the fighter must be indoctrinated with the belief that he is defending his religion and way of life. ASL urges Muslims to accept the scholar Ahmad Shaker's decree that "any cooperation with the British [or in the current case, the Americans], no matter how small, is tantamount to unbridled apostasy…"

Thus, for reasons already stated, Muslims must be in a constant state of war with the United States. In the context of Libya, ASL believes the country is suffering from "humiliation and disgrace" because it abandoned "governing with Islamic Sharia." By adopting a Western-style parliamentary system and not a Sharia-based one, the Libyan government is essentially "fighting Islam." Like the post-Saddam and post-Salih governments in Iraq and Yemen, respectively, post-Qaddafi Libya is attempting to adhere to Western standards of governance.

Indeed, while dawa has been ASL's main focus, it has also taken part in hisbah (enjoining right and forbidding wrong; usually connoting vigilante activities) and jihad. With regard to hisbah, ASL's Zahawi admitted that his group has been involved in the demolition of Sufi shrines and places of worship. Furthermore, ASL stormed the European School in Benghazi and confiscated books on the human body it deemed "pornographic," and thus contrary to Islam. Intimidated, teachers at the school blacked out those sections depicting the human body. In one video, members of Ansar al-Sharia in Sirte whipped some alleged transgressors of Sharia tens of times. Moreover, there have been numerous unsolved assassinations of security officials, government officials and civil society activists, many of which are suspected to be the work of ASL.

ASL's most well-known act of jihad is its attack on the United States consulate in Benghazi. Although there was no formal claim of responsibility, the ambiguous language used in the initial statement by ASL's spokesman, Hani al-Mansuri, suggests that some ASL members participated in the assault. As Mansuri carefully put it, "Katibat Ansar al-Sharia [in Benghazi] as a military did not participate formally/officially and not by direct orders." It is likely that some of ASL's local allies in other militias were involved, too.

On a more regional scale, similar to the Iraq jihad, Libya has become a training hub for those seeking jihad in Syria. In fact, most of those whotrain in Libyan camps – suspected in Misrata, Benghazi, the desert area near Hon and in the Green Mountains in the east – come from thecountries surrounding Libya.

There is increasing proof that ASL is training individuals to fight in Syria. On August 6, 2013, two videos leaked online of Tunisians who had been detained by locals in the Derna region and interrogated. Based on the information in the videos, the footage is likely from the late spring or early summer of 2012. It seems ASL was already actively training fighters for Syria, an ominous fact considering what transpired in Benghazi on September 11, 2012.

Furthermore, members of AST less interested in dawa are likely preparing and training in Libya in preparation for a potential insurgency or terrorism in Tunisia. For example, one Tunisian who had trained in Libya was responsible for an unsuccessful suicide bombing at a beach resort in Sousse, a city southeast of Tunis, in October 2013.

While hisbah and foreign fighter training has continued in the shadowsover the past few years, ASL's war with General Haftar has taken on a more public face, both in its messaging and online content dimensions. Since General Haftar announced Operation Dignity on May 17, thenature of ASL's public presentation has been more of a jihad-first than a dawa-first approach. In late May 2014, at the outset of the conflict, Zahawi held an off therecord press briefing in which he denounced General Haftar and labeled his offensive a crusade against Islam.

Zahawi's comments identified the United States, Saudi Arabia, United Arab Emirates and Egypt as backers of General Haftar, allowing Zahawi to allude to past outside interventions in Afghanistan, Iraq and Somalia and warn the United States against joining the battle. Zahawi struck a defiant tone, asserting that ASL was winning: "We thank God that we were able to defeat Haftar and we challenge him to attempt entering Benghazi again.

We warn him that if he continues this war against us, Muslims from across the world will come to fight, as is the case in Syria right now. The war would continue and Ansar al-Sharia would decide when it ends. "Ever since, ASL's propaganda has cast the residents of Benghazi as victims of aggression. For example, in a video dated May 31, 2014, one interviewee bemoans the destruction of his house and property, which had been shelled by General Haftar's forces. One month later, on July 29, ASL released a video telling the story of how General Haftar's army bombed the people of Benghazi while ASL stood in valiant defense of the city. On August 7, ASL released footage of yet more destruction, with buildings burning and neighborhoods destroyed; on December 1, ASL publicized a series of pictures of burnt out apartments and homes in the Sabri neighborhood of Benghazi. The cumulative intent of these moves, of course, was to shape the war of public opinion against General Haftar.

Beyond fully mobilizing and militarizing ASL in Benghazi, the war united a number of Islamist factions under the banner of Majlis Shura Thuwar Benghazi (MSTB, the Benghazi Revolutionaries Consultative Council). On June 20, 2014, ASL, Raf Allah al-Sahati Brigade, February 17th Martyrs Brigade, Libya Shield 1, and Jaysh al-Mujahidin announced their alliance. MSTB designated ASL's Zahawi as its leader, with Wisam bin Hamid of Libya Shield 1 as the military leaderand Jalal Makhzum of Raf Allah al-Sahati Brigade serving as the military commander.

To this day, MSTB remains a potent force, with its leaders releasing joint videos, as on October 5, when bin Hamid stated, *"[w]e advise [Haftar's army] to return from what they are doing and that they repent to Allah the mighty before it is too late."* Zahawi added, gleefully: *"I congratulate our people in Benghazi on this great victory, and we wish to remain until we complete the phase we are in, and this is to control Benghazi, and God willing it will be safer for its sons and its people."*

Since December 12, ASL has expanded its operations beyond Benghazi to Derna, in part due to its commitments with another newly-created umbrella organization. Indeed, ASL joined the Abu Salim Martyrs Brigade and Jaysh al-Islami al-Libi under the banner of MajlisShura al-Mujahidin Derna (MSMD, the Derna Mujahidin Consultative Council).

Unlike in Benghazi, ASL does not have leading positions in this alliance, highlighting its weaker position in Derna. Instead, the head of the Abu Salim Martyrs Brigade, Salim Dirby, leads MSMD with ASL's Sufyan bin Qumu positioned as a military commander alongside Yusuf bin Tahir of Jaysh al-Islami al-Libi. While in Benghazi the Majlis is fighting General Haftar, the umbrella in Derna in addition to fighting Haftar is also in direct competition with Majlis Shura Shabab al-Islam (MSSI), which pledged baya (fealty) to ISIS and its leader, Abu Bakr al-Baghdadi.

While Libya has become a key jihadi battleground, it has not exacted the same gravitational pull on foreign fighters as the conflict in Syria. However, Libyan training camps are now producing some fighters, initially intended for Syria, who are instead joining up with ASL or the Islamic State in Libya (ISL). The majority of foreign fighters in Libya are from the surrounding countries of

Tunisia, Egypt, Algeria, Sudan and Morocco, but they also include some fighters from Palestine, Saudi Arabia and Yemen.

Similar to other conflict zones, most notably Syria, it seems that the upstart wilayat (provinces) that ISIS has "annexed" in Libya have recently drawn supporters from ASL. In part, this is due to the perception that ISIS is winning, has momentum, and is the "cool" jihadi group. Another likely blow to ASL is the death of Zahawi, which was confirmed in January 2015, even if he had been wounded and out of sight since late October 2014.

The quick rise of MSSI illustrates the changing nature of jihadism in Libya, but generally across the Arab world there has been a split between factions aligned with al-Qaeda and those closer to ISIS. MSSI publicly announced its existence on April 4, 2014, when masked members of the group took to the streets of Derna wearing military uniforms, driving pickup trucks and brandishing rocket-propelled grenade launchers, machine guns and anti-aircraft cannons.

They loudly proclaimed the imposition of Sharia. Until it formally announced allegiance to ISIS, MSSI was involved in such activities as security patrols and guarding the al-Huraysh hospital in Derna. They also publicized those who would "repent" to their cause, confiscated drugs and alcohol, and executed individuals.

In the lead up to ISIS formally "annexing" territory and turning MSSI into Wilayat al-Barqah, MSSI released a statement on June 22, 2014 in support of ISIS and Baghdadi. The statement was followed by a formal declaration of allegiance on October 3 that ceded MSSI's territory in Derna to the caliphate. In honor of the occasion, MSSI organized a forum at al-Sahaba mosque called khilafah ala manhaj al-nabawiyah (the Caliphate upon the methodology of the Prophet), a slogan used by ISIS over the past few years.

A month and a half later, Baghdadi released an audio message declaring the creation of new "provinces" in various Arab countries, including Libya. This conferred new legitimacy upon MSSI, which would operate within three Libyan provinces: Wilayat al-Barqah in the east, Wilayat Fizzan in the south, and Wilayat al-Tarabulus in the west. Highlighting the change, ISIS took control of MSSI's media operations.

Since then, ISL has slowly expanded its writ across different parts of Libya, executing and beheading members of General Haftar's forces along the way. Since the beginning of 2015, ISL has been involved in fighting in Benghazi, Sirte and Derna. It may also have executed two secular Tunisian journalists and killed twenty-one Egyptian Christian hostages in areas around Sirte as well as conducted a terrorist attack against the Corinthia Hotel in Tripoli. While in Sirte and Derna, it has stepped up its hisbah patrols in local markets to ensure that they are not selling rotten or spoiled foods, confiscated hookahs (and closed stores selling tobacco since they view it as against Islam) and ordered stores to suspend sales during daily prayers. It has also conducted some dawa activities, the largest on November 25, 2014 under the motto of "The Caliphate upon the Manhaj [methodology] of the Prophet."

Additionally, it is also providing aid to the poor and needy and giving gifts and sweets to children in Benghazi in order to curry favor. In a move similar to Syria, ISL is now attempting to impose regulations on pharmacies and locals in the health industry. Of course, this shouldn't be interpreted as Islamic State taking full control of Libya, or even any of these cities, but it does highlight its growing presence and prestige.

These developments appear to be eroding ASL's legitimacy as well as its closely guarded and painstakingly manicured reputation. In response, in late January 2015 ASL began trotting out its new Islamic police force and Sharia court in Benghazi. Quite possibly, ASL feels compelled to compete openly with ISL, especially as it loses members to ISL.

This could lead to eventual violence between the two groups similar to what occurred between Jabhat al-Nusra and ISIS in Syria. As of now, there has not been any internecine jihadi fighting. In fact, there are rumors that ASL could pledge allegiance to ISL soon, especially in light of ASL's Sharia official Abu 'Abd Allah al-Libi pledging baya to Baghdadi.

Furthermore, can ASL sustain operations in cities beyond its Benghazi base? It is too early to tell, but if the current trajectory continues, ISL might swallow up ASL recruits outside of Benghazi and even make inroads within the city itself. Jihadi organizations, including ASL, have always been nimble and adaptable; as we have seen with Jabhat al-Nusra, they have been able to survive the challenge from ISIS. For now, however, ASL faces an uncertain future and the prospect of cooptation by ISL or decline.

Islamic State and al-Qaeda in Tunisia

Over the past month, there are increasing signs that The Islamic State (IS) intends to build a base and set up a new wilayah (province) in Tunisia in the near future named Wilayat Ifriqiya, a medieval name for the region of Tunisia (as well as northwest Libya and northeast Algeria). This would challenge al-Qaeda in the Islamic Maghrib's (AQIM) Tunisian branch Katibat 'Uqba ibn Nafi's (KUIN) monopoly on insurgency and terrorism since their campaign in Jebel Chambi began in December 2012, opening another front in the broader AQ-IS war. As a consequence, outbidding between these two adversaries could lead to an escalation in violence, with Bardo National Museum style attacks becoming more common.

In mid-December last year, IS directed its first overt message to the Tunisian state and its people. Aboubaker el-Hakim (who went by Abu al-Muqatil in the video) claimed responsibility for the assassination of Tunisia's secular leftist politicians in 2013 -- "Yes, tyrants, we're the ones who killed Chokri Belaid and Mohamed Brahmi" -- thus confirming the Ennahda-led government's suspicions that he was involved. Beyond calling for more violence and for Tunisians to remember its imprisoned brothers and sisters, he also called upon the Tunisian people to pledge bay'a to Abu Bakr al-Baghdadi, to raise the banner of tawhid (pure monotheism) and to rip down the flags of Charles de Gaulle and Napoleon (alluding to the historically close relations between Tunisia and France).

This was followed on April 7th by Abu Yahya al-Tunisi of IS's Wilayat Tarabulus in Libya, who urged Tunisians to travel to Libya for training in order to establish and extend the writ of IS back at home. Only two days later, a new media account, Ajnad al-Khilafah bi-Ifriqiya (Soldiers of the Caliphate in Ifriqiya) Media Foundation, was created. While unofficial, it foreshadowed the targeting of Tunisia in much the same way the establishment of al-'Urwah al-Wuthqa (The Indissoluble Link) Media foreshadowed the pledge of bay'a given by Boko Haram to IS in March 2015.

Besides IS's claim of responsibility for the Bardo National Museum attack (which the government actually believes KUIN was responsible for), Ajnad al-Khilafah bi-Ifriqiya Media announced IS's first claim of responsibility for an insurgent attack in Jebel al-Meghila, near the town of Sbeitla. Additionally, Ajnad al-Khilafah bi-Ifriqiya Media claimed responsibility on April 22 for a separate attack in Jebel Salloum, in which one of its Algerian fighters was killed (signaling to Tunisians as well that other nationalities were within its ranks.) This was followed by IS official media disseminators, including Ajnad al-Khilafah bi-Ifriqiya Media, claiming responsibility for attacks in Tunisia on

May 2, also in Jebel Salloum. This increasingly formalized approach suggests that the official announcement of a new wilayah may be imminent.

Although KUIN was first identified as a Tunisian cut-out for AQIM in December 2012 by then Tunisian Interior Minister Ali Larayedh, it was not until mid-January 2015 that the battalion publicly acknowledged the association. This pledge was reaffirmed by KUIN following the death of its leader Khalid Shaaib (Abu Sakhr Lukman) in late March and was an attempt to consolidate strength following false rumours that the KUIN might switch sides to IS. These rumors emanated in part from a statement by KUIN showing support for IS though there was no indication of bay'a. The need to distinguish between general support and a religiously-binding pledge of allegiance is vital -- AQAP released a statement in support of IS in Iraq after the fall of Mosul last year.

KUIN has also identified with Ansar al-Sharia in Tunisia (AST) when announcing martyrs, highlighting how some of its fighters are former members. AST has become largely defunct however, with members either being arrested, going abroad to fight and train in Syria and Libya, or joining up with KUIN followings its designation by the Tunisian government as a terrorist organization in late August 2013.

Since it first entered the public gaze, KUIN has remained obscure, maintaining a low-level insurgency with the Tunisian military for 2.5 years in Jebel Chambi. Members have also been arrested for attempted attacks in different cities of Tunisia as well as for weapons smuggling. More recently it has increased its online profile, at first through the Fajr al-Qayrawan Facebook and Twitter account and then Ifriqiya Media, a well-known non-partisan aggregator of online jihadi releases from all African-based jihadi organizations. Only this past weekend, KUIN created an official media outlet for itself called al-Fatih (the conqueror). Up until then, the main content it released showed pictures of its fighters, martyrs, training camps, graphics with quotes from the Qur'an and ghana'im (spoils of war) from its past operation in Hanchir Ettala.

While KUIN has been involved in a low-level insurgency for 2.5 years, it has not altered the status quo in Tunisia. Therefore, if IS attempts a full-scale terrorist or insurgent campaign in Tunisia, pressure on KUIN could mount and an outbidding scenario of escalating violence could ensue. It could also put more pressure on the Tunisian state, which has up to now been able to maintain control against jihadis since the revolution.

That said it is possible one or both organizations might attempt a large-scale attack that would gain a huge media audience, given the onset of tourist season. Moreover, in the aftermath of the Bardo National Museum attack, supporters of

IS flipped the popular meme #IWillComeToTunisiaThisSummer in support of the Tunisian tourism industry on its head by showing off with bullets and weapons, intimating that they too would be coming to Tunisia this summer. Vigilance from both the state and the public, then, will be vital in maintaining order and diminishing the effects of violence.

The Islamic State in Sirte, Libya

While much of the focus on the Islamic State in Libya (ISL) has centered on its mid-June defeat in Darnah, over the past few months it has slowly built up its assets and capabilities in the country's Sirte district. In many ways, this effort is the first example of ISL fully resembling its ISIS parent in Iraq and Syria. Unlike in Darnah, where ISL originated, no other insurgent factions remain in Sirte to compete with the group. This is due to several developments: defections from the local wing of jihadist group Ansar al-Sharia in Libya (ASL), arrangements ISL has made with local tribes, and ex-Qadhafi loyalists from the late leader's hometown joining up with or acquiescing to ISL's rise in Sirte, in a manner similar to ex-Baathists in Iraq. As a result, Sirte could soon become the capital for ISL, equivalent to Raqqa in Syria and Mosul in Iraq.

Because ISL co-opted the ASL network in Sirte, convincing it to pledge *baya* (allegiance) to ISIS leader Abu Bakr al-Baghdadi in late fall 2014, it did not have to start from scratch when establishing itself in the area. Sirte was the first city in which ASL operated outside its base in Benghazi, beginning in late June 2013. For example, it put on a Quranic competition for Ramadan in July 2013, in association with the local Office of Awqaf, Radio Tawhid, the Cleaning Services Company, and the University of Sirte; a year later, it cosponsored a Ramadan *dawa* event with al-Baynah Foundation. This illustrated that ASL had been preparing to establish itself in Sirte ahead of time and had ties to key players within the city.

From that point forward, Sirte became ASL's second-busiest hub. The group was involved in a variety of governance, *hisba* (accountability), and *dawa* (proselytizing) activities in the area, at times extending them into other parts of the Gulf of Sidra region such as al-Nawfaliyah and Bin Jawad.

On the governance front, ASL provided security patrols in various neighborhoods and the University of Sirte, helped arbitrate issues between tribes and clans (including some from faraway Misratah), returned a stolen ambulance to a hospital, regulated traffic, and cleaned roads, among other things. In terms of *hisba* -- the system by which an Islamic "state" is entrusted with commanding right and forbidding wrong -- the group implemented the *tazir* penalty (i.e., corporal and other punishments left to the discretion of the authorities, as distinct from punishments set by the Quran) and confiscated and destroyed drugs, cigarettes, and alcohol. It was also involved in providing *iftar* (breaking of the fast) tents and supplying presents to children during Ramadan, as well as giving lessons on how to circumambulate the Kaaba correctly during the Hajj in Mecca, passing out slaughtered sacrificial animals during Eid al-Adha, providing school supplies at the beginning of the school year, converting foreign workers to Islam, and conducting charity drives for needy families.

All of this illustrates that when ISL began moving into Sirte, there was already a strong apparatus in place to exploit. The city now provides the perfect environment for ISL to build itself up in Libya.

ISL originated in Darnah in April 2014, when it called itself Majlis Shura Shabab al-Islam. After the Abu Salim Martyrs Brigade (former members of the Libyan Islamic Fighting Group) kicked the group out of Darnah in mid-June 2015, Sirte became the main priority for its state-building enterprise. Yet ISL had already been building up its presence in Sirte and other key cities in the district, including al-Nawfaliyah and Harawa. The group drew support from ASL defectors in Sirte as early as October 2014, but it did not act publicly inside the city until early January, from its base at the Ouagadougou Conference Center. Sirte was also the site where ISL members murdered Egyptian Christians in mid-February and Ethiopian Christians in mid-April.

ISL's campaign to seize full control of Sirte was jumpstarted on February 8, 2015, when it took over al-Nawfaliyah some ninety miles to the east. Apparently, ASL defectors provided logistical support for ISL members to enter the city; after securing it, ISL called for residents to pledge *baya* to Baghdadi and named Ali Qarqa (a.k.a. Abu Hamam al-Libi) as the town's new leader. This provided the group with its first true base in the broader Sirte district. Since then, it has focused on numerous activities in al-Nawfaliyah: conducting outreach forums; destroying cigarettes, alcohol, and caches of what ISL deems "sorcery materials"; distributing *dawa* leaflets; and training new soldiers.

The week after the al-Nawfaliyah takeover, ISL began making bolder moves in Sirte city, taking the radio station, the Wataniya television studio, the immigration center, Ibn Sina Hospital, the University of Sirte, and local government buildings. By then it controlled more than half of the city and had installed a local leader: Usamah Karamah, a relative of a former senior Qadhafi intelligence officer.

This led the Misratan faction called the Fajr 166 Brigade to launch a counter-campaign aimed at retaking the city, but the effort failed because many leaders back in Misratah were incredulous at the time that ISL had actually infiltrated Sirte and viewed the fight with Gen. Khalifa Haftar in the east as a higher priority. In late May, ISL seized al-Qardabiya Air Base and the Great Man-Made River irrigation complex; then, on June 9, it took the city's power plant, giving it complete control of Sirte. Afterward, ISL members began to loot and destroy the homes of local politicians.

The next week, ISL took over Harawa, halfway between Sirte and al-Nawfaliyah. This move consolidated the group's hold over a swath of territory stretching around 125 miles. ISL has shown little sign of governance activities in Harawa so far, focusing instead on handing out *dawa* leaflets and CDs, destroying cigarettes and other items the group deems *haram* (forbidden), distributing *zakat al-fitr* (charity given to the poor at the end of Ramadan), allegedly liberating a number of Egyptian Muslim prisoners kidnapped by "corrupted" bandits, and in one case arresting a thief.

ISL has also taken other towns such as al-Wushka (about sixty-five miles west of Sirte city) and Wadi Zamzam (105 miles west). The latter town extends into Misratah district, suggesting that wider fighting could emerge between ISL and the Misratans -- thus far they have only issued empty threats against ISL.

ISL's operations in Sirte have grown more sophisticated since June, surpassing even its original efforts in Darnah -- a situation abetted by its current lack of competition. Prior to June, the vast majority of its activities were limited to *dawa* and *hisba*: distributing literature, conducting forums, converting Christians, implementing *tazir* and *hudoud* (punishments for crimes against God that are based on the Quran and hadith, such as flogging, stoning, amputation, and execution), and demolishing shrines, among other activities described above.

After ISL's Darnah defeat and Sirte expansion, many members went west to help consolidate the group's control and governance efforts there. Although it still engages in *dawa* and *hisba*, ISL is now in the state-building stage -- it aims to show residents that life is continuing and that its presence has brought normalcy and stability. Similar efforts were seen last fall in Iraq and Syria, where ISIS members ostentatiously placed the group's black flag on lamp posts, erected *dawa* billboards throughout towns, conducted tours of different industries, highlighted the group's public works projects, and publicized photos showing the beauty and peacefulness of life in the so-called "Caliphate."

Likewise, ISL members in Sirte have shown off the city's landscapes, port, bustling markets, and fully stocked grocery stores. They have also decorated the entrance to the city with ISL flags, installed numerous *dawa* billboards, cleaned and decorated streets, provided *zakat* to the needy, visited Ibn Sina hospital, and toured local brick, aluminum, marble, and milk factories.

In another parallel to Iraq and Syria, ISL members have called on individuals to join the group's ranks via video messages issued under the aegis of "Wilayat Tarabulus," the so-called ISIS "province" encompassing northwestern Libya. In late January, Abu Umar al-Tawrigi called on his fellow Tuaregs to join the group and pledge *baya* to Baghdadi. In late April, Abu Muhammad al-Ansari stated, "Come to Libya. Our hearts and homes are open to you." In early June, Abu Dujana al-Sudani urged potential recruits to make *hijra* (emigrate) to ISL. And last month, Abu Hamza al-Masri reiterated these entreaties, asking legal scholars in particular to come help the group implement sharia.

ISL's seizure of Sirte has given the Islamic State a more sustainable base than its failed attempts in Darnah, as well as its first capital outside Iraq and Syria. Whether this leads to further territorial gains remains to be seen, especially given the various rivalries and areas of influence among Libya's many factions.

But ISL will become a far more formidable force if it is able to link its territory in Sirte district to the central Jufrah district, which has the Mabruk oil field and the town of Waddan -- a key supply line for Fajr between Misratah and Sebha districts and a pivotal crossroads for various criminal networks that ISL hopes to take over. The group is also attempting to co-opt more pro-Qadhafi tribes in the Fezzan region further south.

Meanwhile, ISL's consolidation has led ASL -- which still operates independently in Benghazi and to a lesser extent Ajdabiya and Darnah -- to focus more on service provision, dispensing justice, and security. This could lead to an eventual bidding war between the two rival jihadist groups. Whatever the case, it is important for U.S. policymakers and other parties to understand that while ISL did indeed lose in Darnah, it has emerged even stronger in Sirte.

The Tunisian-Libyan Jihadi Connection

It should have come as no surprise that Seifeddine Rezgui, the individual who attacked tourists in Sousse, Tunisia, more than a week ago, had trained at a camp in Libya. The attack represented the continuation of a relationship between Tunisian and Libyan militants that, having intensified since 2011, goes back to the 1980s. The events in Sousse are a stark reminder of this relationship: a connection that is set to continue should the Islamic State (IS) choose to repeat attacks in Tunisia in the coming months.

Although Ennahda did not explicitly call for individuals to fight against the Soviets during the Afghan jihad, militants in the mujahedeen were regularly involved in facilitation and logistical networks that brought Libyans to the region. Additionally, according to Noman Benotman, a former shura council member of the Libyan Islamic Fighting Group (LIFG) in Afghanistan in the 1980s, Libyans alongside Abdul Rasul Sayyaf, the Afghan leader of Ittihad-e-Islami, attempted to help the Tunisians create their own military camp and organization. This would not come to fruition until 2000, when future leaders of Ansar al-Sharia in Tunisia (AST), Tarek Maaroufi (based in Brussels) and Sayf Allah Bin Hassine (moved from London to Jalalabad, Afghanistan; also known as Abu Iyadh al-Tunisi), cofounded the Tunisian Combatant Group.

Following the Afghan jihad, many Ennahda members were exiled to Europe in the late 1980s and early 1990s by former president Ben Ali. While some returned home, the committed were drawn to the jihadi and foreign fighter networks that had spread across Europe, especially in Milan, Italy. Milan became a central hub for recruitment, logistics, and facilitation of foreign fighters going to the Bosnian war as well as assisting the Armed Islamic Group (GIA) in the Algerian jihad.

While the Egyptian Anwar Shaaban led the network, the group surrounding him was made up largely of Tunisians and Libyans, with some Algerians and Moroccans, working together. This milieu helped build interesting relationships among the individuals, along with other cells in Europe. One in particular was between Sami Essid bin Khamis, a future leader of AST, and the Libyan Lased Ben Heni, who was based in Frankfurt, who worked together to plan the 2000 Strasbourg Cathedral Plot (along with the London Algerian jihadi network).

Following 9/11, the successor group to the GIA in Algeria was the Groupe Salafiste pour la Predication et le Combat (GSPC; which would eventually become al-Qaeda in the Islamic Maghrib in 2007). In 2003, Nabil Sahrawi, the leader at the time, was attempting to regionalize the jihad beyond Algerian borders and emphasize recruitment from Tunisia and Libya. While the organization was still dominated by Algerians, the Tunisians and Libyans worked together in GSPC's "Zone 5," which was close to the border with Tunisia and under the banner of El-Fatah El-Moubine.

Because of this, there were a number of cases in the mid to late 2000s where groups of Algerians, Tunisians, and Libyans would get arrested together, either on the Algerian or Tunisian side of their respective borders. In many ways, this formation was a precursor to the now AQIM splinter group Katibat Uqba ibn Nafi (KUIN), based in the Chaambi Mountains on the Tunisian-Algerian border. Around the same time, GSPC networks in Algeria and remnant LIFG networks in Libya were providing logistics and facilitation to fighters going to Iraq in the mid-2000s to fight with al-Qaeda (the precursor to IS). There were a number of routes that Tunisians took to get to Iraq, but one was through the Libyan support networks, which was a reversal of the 1980s trend.

Here many relationships were forged, which would be important after 2011 since a number of Iraq jihad veterans then became involved with AST, Ansar al-Sharia in Libya (ASL), and then eventually the Islamic State in Libya. One such case was Abu Radwan al-Tunisi, from Bizerte, who came to Iraq via Libya and eventually died fighting the Badr Brigades.

Over the past four years, many of the prior trends continued and, at times, accelerated, in reaction to the opening up of Tunisian society and to Libya becoming a relative safe haven for foreign militants. AQIM continued to play a role, especially with smuggling weapons through Tunisia from Libya. Therefore, as with the last decade, a number of Tunisian and Libyan AQIM members have been arrested on Tunisian or Libyan soil, either together or by themselves, in relation to smuggling or plotting terrorist attacks set to occur on: May 2011, June 2011, February 2012, February 2012, December 2012, May 2013, May 2013, June 2013, May 2014, May 2014, June 2014, August 2014, August 2014, and August 2014. Then, in the fall of 2014, more people got arrested for similar reasons, except this time with relation to IS: September 2014, October 2014, December 2014, March 2015, and June 2015.

Besides the many arrests (of which many were likely not made public), there was also a strengthening relationship between Tunisian and Libyan militants through their sister organizations Ansar al-Sharia in Tunisia and Libya. ASL learned from the AST dawa model, with Tunisians providing assistance on how to implement it. There were already signs that Tunisians were training in Libya as early as the spring of 2012. These camps are likely where the original failed Sousse suicide bomber of October 2013 trained.

Within Libya, many attacks against Tunisian diplomatic facilities, such as against its embassy and twice against its consulate in June 2012, were connected with ASL. There is even the case of the Tunisian Ali Ani al-Harzi, who was recently killed in an American airstrike in Iraq fighting for IS. He was one of the ringleaders of the infamous Benghazi U.S. Consulate attack in September 2012, which is most associated with ASL.

Moreover, following the Tunisian government's designation of AST in late August 2013, those who did not quit the movement, get arrested, or join up with the jihad in Syria or with KUIN in the Chaambi Mountains, fled to Libya and ASL, including AST's leader, Abu Iyadh al-Tunisi. Further, as a result of the breakdown in AST, a short-lived integration between Tunisian and Libyan militant networks took place through the rebranding of AST to Shabab al-Tawhid.

Beyond the AST and ASL networks, since the fall of 2014, there has been increased Tunisian activity in Libya with IS. According to the Tunisian government, it is believed that up to 1,000 Tunisians are currently fighting or training in Libya. Even as dozens of Tunisians have died on the battlefield in Libya, a Tunisian was one of the attackers of the Corinthia Tripoli Hotel in late January 2015.

Additionally, a number of these Tunisian IS operatives have been dispatched back home and been involved in a spate of low-level insurgent attacks since early April 2015. Of course, most recently the two most high-profile attacks in Tunisia, first in March at the Bardo Museum in Tunis and less than two weeks ago at the beach resorts in Sousse, were all trained in Libya, at the same camps, by IS.

Therefore, with the continued Tunisian government security concerns as well as the difficulty in securing the Tunisian-Libyan border over the past four years, it is likely that we will see future IS attacks that emanate from or are connected with Libya. What we have seen already did not come out of nowhere; it has a history that stretches back decades and represents a problem too often ignored, taken lightly, or blamed on others by Tunisian officials prior to and after the 2011 revolution.